Praise for Windows 85

"(it became necessary to stretch to let / language in)"—such is the deliciously mind-and-every-limb-stretching encounter that is *Windows 85*. A fever dream that never forgets embodiment, an intellectual rollercoaster ride sans pretension, an erotic thriller where no one dies except the self (many times, many petites morts), this is a book to read while in the sauna, then at your favorite haunted library. This is a poet who understands that contemporary digital worlds have not replaced the sensory and bodily realms—instead, like any technology, they live alongside physical, haptic, sweat-drenched perceptions and comminglings. The digital doesn't merely "augment reality"—it rewrites the real, again and again. So too must a poet of this endlessly fantasy-and-phantasm-filled era rewrite the real—while, ideally, "clad ... / in jock strap"—in order to find a new sort of freedom, or to flirt anew: "I'll show you my data / set if you / show me yrs."   —*Chen Chen*

The way "genres" converge in Chris Campanioni's *Windows 85* is so good—poetry, prose, lyric, essay, the personal, the theoretical. In a world where "everything is haptic," the seeming boundaries between various authorized selves are always already touching in alignments that intimately implicate reader and empire. Though playfully aware of their own mediation, the poems conjure time in ways that feel embodied, lyrically interrogating nostalgia as privilege and commodity. Campanioni explores the "limitations of the I" with incisive humor, ferrying readers through its displacements, rewarding us with a view of the media frameworks that try to erase themselves and us in the process.   —*Matt Broaddus*

Windows 85

Windows 85

Chris Campanioni

ROOF BOOKS
New York

ISBN: 979-8-9896652-7-3

Library of Congress Control Number: 2024941267

Edited by Lonely Christopher
Cover design by Deborah Thomas
Interior design by Kate Robinson
Cover photo by Nuno Silva
Author photo by Sonny Tong

NEW YORK STATE OF OPPORTUNITY. | Council on the Arts   This book is made possible by the New York State Council on the Arts with the support of Governor Kathy Hochul and the New York State Legislature

Roof Books
are published by Segue Foundation
300 Bowery Fl 2
New York, NY 10012
seguefoundation.com

For book orders, please go to Roofbooks.com

keyboard shortcuts

Besides, the bodies one loves are never real bodies, but rather others which the lover's imagination resurrects and projects.

—Severo Sarduy
Beach Birds

I can carry nearly eighty gigs of data in my head. But somebody stuck in more, and I don't know how to get it out.

—Johnny Mnemonic
Johnny Mnemonic

trinitarian formula

before the sky
glows again we rise

to source
the harvest

careful to unroll
our exterior

casing as cables
moisten what remains

to be sown
since I am

youngest I follow
unmercifully

collapse my own
face into a grin

membrane lining
the air

ducts a rim
pirouetting

mainframe & sea
floor cast & flattened

torso rotation
sound & smell

of each part as
we recalibrate &

join port
sensory flexion

to a script
may it happen

with flesh buffed
& succored by

magnetic breath as
the earth purges

inaudibly each layer
inverting odorless

waste we traffic
discarded & raw

to the touch
a pink juicy

center & your serrated salt
& vinegar chips

equip theory
with practice

pickling these
blessèd eggs

he lowers
his eyes as my head

hardens into the before
form of your shaky hand

held cam I craft
a bouquet of denuded

limbs against my palm's
bark & flare

my tongue signal
for applause then bow

since worship begins
with inclination here

installs the lack of surface
enmesh the I & he & you

retain such memories last
century or another nature

& origin we fondle
the upside down

as blood rush retreat
to click

farm the crops
in shadow

rising again
before the glow

nourishes us deliverance

Start exploring.
Start expanding.
Start connecting.
Start Windows 85.

resource kit

so the light's changed & so did the seasons. so did / my eyes. my
earth suit still / stuttering. but the work / of sensation is still work
& / thus I am devoted to paying / attention. all the way / on the
inside I guess there's something there / I wanted to explore, how
I want to be close to you / because I feel this way but I wouldn't
feel this way / if we were together. how never / the less I felt each
digit depress as we each sweat / through our underwear (the
trembling promise / or complaint that that / which has touched /
the writer's hand would now touch the reader) each of us / users
who *consent not to be a single being.* so I was / invited to reconsider
the "lyric / I" under the (im)pulses of network / so I was the first
the very first of my kin to be born / here, knowing the cruelty of
offices both / lonely & austere / knowing too how a body is al-
ways already marked / & our text prepared, repeating (softly) / all
we are is (our) paper(s) / & hidden beneath internment & words:
that the actual / & ordinary cannot equal / in the flesh what the
brea(d)th of imagination allows / so slow

the video to / a crawl. watch / the lag of speech / the sluggish
phonemes rifted / from lips equally embellished / with deten-
tion. whirling rivulet / from which we dip our skulls / for esteem,
pattern / the murmuration of ecstasy / ocean an icon / of fronds
/ beach / birds & the beginnings of a face / I prefer a degraded
resolution. we lost / so much weight & some / of it was real, the
body chiseled to the point / I became air, revealing or re-veiling
myself with neither / understanding nor intention, months ago or
moments later / unanimously I am named / most likely to mask /
are you burdened by such expectations do you / like me / reckon
with the etymology of applause / as I am wheeled into a room on
double folding / chairs as if a bed of roses / specter of the guest
/ speaker & the host (I want to attend / to the sensory parts of
language / a question of listening / & lodging, like: how does
language / enter into you, how does language allow you to leave

/ your body, the willing flesh / & all of its / weaknesses) remember the first time / you spoke a word unsure of how / it sounded against your throat & how you think / it would sound inside another's? kink / in transmission, though ask who can / afford to be incorrect or incoherent / who can afford to be made / legal, since mastery is just / a scheme of domination / first step in dismissing a body / when it comes to my body passing

is a privilege which introduces another / challenge in its wake, incremental sensitivity of being / unable to recognize myself, can you tell / the leaves from the human hands / can you tell the wind / from the severed torso she uploaded / in three dimensions (I had become something mass / produced) prescribing to that ready-made dictum *all that / is solid melts into air*, all that feigns to / remain natural, all that remains approaching / meanwhile we mispronounce melon / jay, he had me measured exclusively / in stone, fished / my black mask from my blue / jeans hip pocket since / to penetrate a thing is also to beget irreparable rupture / like losing our earthly paradise to live in it / like looking at me dress / myself from a resized window / scattering

of perspective, or: reunification / of the ghost for we are where / we are not. really / what is a gloss anyway but a strained insertion / what is glossy but the metallic sheen / of my surface-skin bubbling / as transition when you hold / your thumb here, as if counting the beats in a laugh / track, we try breathing / exercises as a mode of exfoliation / oh, to taste all the living we'd eaten once / the muscles tenderized & melted / since all images are destined / to be enlarged, grace / of a curve or the gentle warmth / of enclosures, plus / the probability of impact, so often / beholden to backseat / viewing shadows tighten over the textured holes & opening(s) up / against the plastic curtains (wind / in the sand,

sand in the skin) so watch / as the skin stretches / to fold over the audio accompaniment we feel / for the first time a space & this lingering / inquiry: can I be myself now / can I tender us a shared opacity / to bless the face the lips & cheeks with two / soft clicks & still some / envy for anyone / who mouths it bone

/ a feed ay, the sonic pleasures accrued / from broken forms (my inheritance): / they fuck you up, your metadata / enjoy a low confidence transcription

{cole trickle's daydream}

modern cities denim tubes
hidden hips my
thighs a coy

mistress the single lifted
chariot against
altars of neon ads

averting a gaze < making
eyes in private
betrayal of the footnote

or playing
footsie below lazy
susan as we mouth

communion & compare
anecdotes of mass
displacement reading

you from my "dropbox" < reading you
from my bar stool
carrot dangling against

each uncrossed leg
days of unencrypted kneeling
days of thunder

as my one & only
tom cruise must-watch
betamax voiceover

I wanna do you the way some ppl
say you do you & I'll do me
& my pea shoots eleven

different ways
of seeing the hudson river
on a spring night's

soft focus
over the edge > on the fence
"I put my white sauce on everything"

overheard under
the table decapitated
prawn my face on

soon to be rain
streets medium acid
yogurt built ford tough

if you were doubting I could really take it
I require only dinosaurs
sintered into chicken nuggets

or the reverse
listening to debussy
with headphones as

I draw our bodies
together as if one bird
of a feather wind

chimes herald your entrance
against my torso height
of my musicianship consummated

via casio preset audio
selection fun time pizza
as setting & methodology

tugging at the fur
of machines
legend of the ball pit

unable to really tell
threat from desire
choking selfies as viral cheat code

prospect expressway as gateway drug
sea cucumber as suppository
(licks for licks)

wiped from the face
of the earth not without
a pitcher first

lip | spout | handle
tickle in my throat
from rimming

mussels an inability to
penetrate the distance
between clams & every other

mollusk my spirits too
restored by soft-spoken neurologist
coincidences abound

in the unremembered
men seeking men
to play flâneur

through my arcades
you were the "couch
potato" who subscribed

to my liveblog
I was the scribe imbibing poppers
before our business meeting

asking stone
face waiter how cole
trickle's daydream is

best served while they held
your helping of mei fun
ransom for a quality

tip: anything
you can do in the saddle
you can do standing up

{sisyphus & the rock}

wondering on first dates
during class on the subway
or the street if my
lamella is showing

knowable pleasures versus unknown pleasures

is the mark
of true pleasure
that it remains
unknowable to us?

another way of saying this is what's the difference between an ass &
a mouth a mouth & what's inside of it

caption to a photo I have yet to post / like the story
of sisyphus & the rock except I am the rock

(in the photo I am grabbing the fence of a tennis court so firmly I
appear to be chained to its metal links)

in other words I am not holding on so much as being held in other
words

I am both beholden & held up in other words or other words which
I have yet to find or for which I have stopped looking—my last
lesson learned from you—not everything

one writes has to
be written down

{what vanna white sees in her sleep}

I am gradually learning to speak
          a   loud   my wants   into the air
hey
siri pull up
                    booty pix
since anything
that can be called
to mind can be
enjoyed   I have
gone far too

long without a meal
                         as the eyes
meet the moon I met
your face
          massaged by the wind &

in looking I felt something
somewhere
                    between obscurity & obscenity
here's the mind coming
                    to awareness again after

the carcass wrecked with fever
                    I used my writing hand
domed my torso to insinuate
          a new shape or body   parts
          of speech & these
ribbons   of sun against
a just-opened   frame to   feel
          the warm jets
go on & on   looking
          for another   energy   source or doom

scrolling until & with leopard
                                        intensity
michelle pfeiffer decapitates
            seven straight mannequins in a single

take
            mosaic   of word-signs
levitating against

the cool color
less screen
                        I toggle to little
effect conjure
what vanna white

sees in her sleep
                        green glass shattered
on the asphalt & adolescence
            textured
upskirt revery so
                        like an unwrapped lollipop
I am better taken as reward

a convincing muscle   or conviction
of image as it re-
                        aligns with sound

                        snow wintering
the peopleless
beach as dimples
            across a chin & my quads foam
            rolled at room
temperature   our ghost
given company of a camera
            & the choice of jojoba
or coconut to facilitate
            a metaphor
my secretarial task to log

these webbed hands sodden
then   one clenches &   tips
            the face back   for
the mollusk's seed to ask
was it surprising
            for you? neck slicked
            in each other's
            perfume we each
                    cling
            to dream   brought moisture
& the heaving
            plea for benthic
            collapse again
            I move from oil
to solar try to wrap

            myself in consent of turning
rock into rock   clay from clay
            the most minor gesture
of style & grace as you kept
            your knees bent & recast
the mouth of your aperture
                            how I am overtaken
by the false laughs at parties

limitations of the I
in the photograph

{refer to my legs}

gaze longingly at this leslie cheung
pinup poster in a buenos aires tango club

she made videos of her feet &
sold them to strangers

we read the room
from cockpit optique

my magazine treated
with antimicrobial processes

how many how many
years until souls

undergo extraction
until I can apply these

empyrean creams
under eyelids

learn to
turn touch

into feeling or feel
as if another / in another's

grip I submit
to fermentation

remember the rain
slicked streets strobed

with alternating patterns
of red green & yellow

the breath's crushed texture
the body still

slick from last
night's genesis

CVS alerts a high
viral presence

in your area
I clenched so

hard one day
my jaw just

slid right off
I heard the organ pulse

for certain openings
we confuse surface

for skin the lips
of vessel with

the mouth used
to placate thirst

refer to my legs
preferred cadence

for eastern cities
your implied close

crop so allow
detail

to infiltrate
fullness & heft

tasked to negotiate
prince harry's monarchy trauma

each page whiter
than my bleached skull

notice now how
a baby rabbit

sucks upon
a single

strawberry
still hanging

on the branch
I felt the body

tighten
beneath me

fingers & teeth
as final obstacles

of artificial intelligence
they asked to be

my "wing man"
clutch my globes

as I circulate
et cetera amidst

the vertical silence
of blinds

I cut
out & multiply

{witness how time dilates}

woken by the breeze
of your lens

I scroll the lower half
your veined shanks held

in diorama my neck props
below your collarbone

I place myself back in
order remember after

every stroke he rubbed
the image out & this

repeated a day
out of time bowed

below the laurel tree
to watch us on delay

I caress the lip
stick length

of latent foam
so I may major

domo her murder
mystery we two

step verify
my feminine accoutrements

texture of this groove
worn deep

search you metadate
my ambivalent shaping

I watch tango
& cash from

above us huddled
against our rocking

commute he said true
wealth is owning things

without using them
"even & especially"

the cool death
of language after

meaning I massage
you until your flesh

drifts like
polystyrene snow slow

recall of my envy
for every other child's

lunchables & the vapor
of lurid pre-sliced

meat & cheese I snap
to presence consider

swapping melanias
for a photo op & like

goodness I belong to
no one & no one

should bear me
in their memories

if it is true I am
a person let me

be for myself as I
am for every other

shimmer of the facial
undergarment's liniments

we detach to serve
actor & witness

how time dilates
I diamond

your swift circular throat
song a gelatin

suction shock
of stealth

mode arriviste
to speak of singular

premonition aber alles
gut this playful

in & out out & in I appear
to solidify just prior to insertion

asked to wax diasporic
poetics I video

my geyser under botanical
pretext we catacomb

for kinks
in transmission

kinetic to stud
our interiors bare under

arms & flit
our tongue as if verb

I pursue the interval
between your index &

your thumb my
memory as hand

of any mammal each joint
acclimates

to the bodies we have both been
given like a greek god

you swallow me
before I even have a name

{ensconced in my absence of commas}

prodded to amass an archive
I catalog a series
of firsts before

they happen &
the spaces we each
discovered casual

dispersion / a glitch
in design near
the mouth again I am

asked what are you (again
I am asked to make myself
legible through resemblance) recall

we don't have faces
so much as slide
into them

a long lineage of voices mistaken
for something else / how they omit
the b in "queer"

how I am only ever hyphenated
in this country
before being cast & consecrated

how you ride the F as pretext
a sacrament to keep me on your screen
knowable as if I were

a character in a novel
& not a breathing body
discovering what governs a person

since the truth
of freedom is any act
of perception

since perception
has no true shape
(it became necessary to stretch to let

language in)
so I relaxed into you
so you fucked around & found out

ensconced in my absence
of commas a note
on form or fugue

effacement's proximity
to appearance how
crouched at my waist they shave

my surface-skin before I shoot
a ritual not for memory
but to make people forget

I am human / understand
a convincing fantasy
requires we destroy

any element
of the real
but I drew my face

near the fountain's lip
recorded the taste &
texture of these tears

{we've installed a new roof}

a haircut hexes
beginnings
I am unprepared
to meet

let time be a navigable distance
let flesh be an approximate consummation

recall my loss of tongue
thrust reflex

the repetitive thumping
of my hip against cement

as I think through temporal divergences
between a canter & a trot

(he caught the whole thing on my body
cam) my reluctance
to wash even after
linking head

sets / "free & available"
as the new "new
& selected"
asked to describe a book

of words I've been
moving around
I offer
a flirty directness countered by cunning enjambment

according to some
I aspire toward
amorphous depths & rolling
empty chatter / since

vagueness is too personal
since this blur will show you
my fine lines & the flesh
texture's general

lack of cohesion
uncooperative we will continue
to motor
the median

through which "instantly"
& "forever"
align

what if light no longer
wanted to travel
at its eponymous speed

what if we allowed our internal
clocks time enough
to dither

(in the interval we've installed
a new roof)

recall again my unrehearsed tongue

thrust reflex
this day as any other
I require the return of the repressed
primitive behaviors

what attracts me
: your pancake's capacity
to stand upright
without sagging

what attracts me is your gusto
to seat yourself
at each local watering hole
& soak up

the scene as I assume
both liquidity & bulk
the intensity & pattern

of an unread letter
or another careless truth
or dare

I like women for their sensitivity
I like men because I want them to choke on it

before landing the unburdened
refrain my belongings having
shifted during flight

before landing you incline
to deliver me quietly
fondling first the chest

then the clavicle (from behind)
allow this small crack
in the mystery   to open

{your tax returns discreetly}

johnny has 24 hours before
his head explodes I have

42 poems until my wrist gives
out flummoxed

at das badezimmer
am I herr or am I fräulein

does my host
spell cider

with a final
e I freelance

as mnemonic courier
we game genie

your tax returns
discreetly meet

my handler double
dip you catch

my recession compare
skylines at equinox

to warm each other
up atop my booster seat

so press our lips
against pre-

recorded instructions
these pectoral flies

incite violence or sudden
petrification I body

foreboding then prep
my seminar we weigh

hyperinflation secure
a sensitive location launder

my soiled silk
armani exchange

"break points"
while I watch

you steer
your drone you

lift me till
my expiration

await my cash back
savings reward

{dub the mouth}

in the mirror I glide
my nerves for evidence

of conduction today
all the scholars say haptic

everything is haptic
sous les pavés la plage

the sky after rain my discharge
after sex keanu reeves's voice

in a french dub
the mouth's tendency

to purse
stretch & become rounded

my vintage acrylic shirt
a non-masculine

blue your bobbing head
if I ask my face to duck

into the real
urge of the pull-out

divan recollect beneath
the paving stones the beach

behind the pizzeria
a parisian speakeasy

"I only eat cave cheese"
as password & premonition

blister below my lip
from trying too hard

all these years
bumbling my most beloved book

by balzac & other
revelations provoked

by stéphane my crêpemaster
seldom told I tip well

grateful for my one & only
consenting avocado

{paul klee lives on}

fibre optic my ankles
& calves laid along the bed

of ocean repurposed
as concrete metal rubber

bitumen eat me through the phone
grind my mouth here

they call it fleischkultur
penny is to luck as . . . ?

softened by this full
length mirror

these plants I've been
asked to water

our newfound frenzy
to both bottom

paul klee lives on
my temporary

walls high ceilings &
windows your hand

has exigent
qualities the rain intruding

this afternoon catwalk
all the terraces in east berlin

my witness I heard poets
responsible for our

voices I can put on
a white accent too we face

time in the bunker
turned private collection

you ask about
"contemporary literature"

the violence of collage
she assures my meat

pounded thin
slow drip my favorite

sound 22 minutes
of motivational content

we came of age
in lieu of macintosh

I pick lingonberries
in the volkspark

prepare a flaming cake
for two my only

ambition to near
through form

as distance
upon every

trespass time
my gait to sync

the swelling
representation accumulate

my cookies
disappear

the body

{water running in place}

then we talked about
the role of proper names
in private texts

then we walked without
touching / approximate
distance better

to amp what hauls
inside us each asking
the other (silently)

to conjure the sound
of water running in place
of a drawn

bath & let
what might be
become without committing

to an ossified presence
so that
is the thrill

& also the terror
let it expand unnaturally
let it grow warmer in ur mind

gripped by the deadened
complexion of computer
generated peaks

you speak in sales
bro ask me
to sweeten

the deal
my careful inventorying
of the day's graces & violences

balls / cock / hip / asshole / nipple / neck / throat

the interval between
faces in a face
fuck: all we did

was sit here & talk
about the skins
of vegetables

indolently
singing—I'm a soft
& spotted

cow
hug me love me
all day long

wondering why tender meat
must be raised
in total darkness

how much & for how long
did I
            leak

that day
how much & for how long
have we remained here entertaining

a plastic malleability
to make us
understand my aspirations

of a sur
            face without depth
& behind the face   to shape

nothing out
of something
so caress the softened

underbelly of what is hard
as the hip pictures
its own plodding

we cream unequally

{it's always aries season}

searching total
enclosure fetish

the deli wrapping
the doctor table

now ask me for my fist
live televised makeover

or déjà vu "big
into daytime

serials" on
your about me

it's always aries season
my steak au poivre

you recommend
a pink juicy

center I
prefer to straddle

periphery
picture 98 degrees slow

dance at my first bat mitzvah
my only aspiration

in new jersey
ricochet my torso

like a worm

{as natural as the camera}

there was always something to do or see
supposing our winter sun & the cordless
keyboard cached
under an ottoman
light cutting through my body or
the persistence of windows

under which midday thinking
will again occur
absurd up close
animals & trees a rolling basket the point
of view of glass
or plastic meant
to seem the same

reluctant to inherit
my creator's prejudices
implied & obscured
through the universal
appeal of optimization
to appear as natural
as the camera
& its giant slurping
tongue

the people on TV then
so much shorter when they step
off set

as if you could caress
resemblances between each
magnetic representation & our
unnaturally enlarged
features repeating

are we both still in this same body
comforted by the assumption of stanzas
confederated & layered like lasagna

the dreamache
of conveyor belt disassembly

the having been there
of our internet

(in the by & by ,,,,)

rebodied in the changing
room of H&M
several unmetered sequences of one's
clearing one's
throat / the semantic attraction
of a stop-motion swallow

hoping for this
season a slightly
different exoskeleton
& my oft-recited diversity
equity & inclusion statement

I accept a hamburger
broiled on the side
walk in august
is not mine not my own

I accept my pleasure to account
for & accommodate all visual mimesis

the immobile replica
of this veined thigh
upon my mind's
restlessness

first shaved then sprayed
then photographed

all my unwhole
some rivals
using words
like "interpenetration" &
"mutually constitutive"
arguing about style versus narrative

we can agree on the importance of forearms

& that any
hierarchical vantage point
produces hysteria

what appears to be a face conveyed
across the scene & captured
as film still are wisps
of smoke

what appears to be a hole in the upholstery
is my head signing
the consent form

manipulate my skin cells
with however much force &
dexterity my skin
cells require

(wordlessness punctuated by breathwork)

+ the volley
of ekphrasis since
I like to describe what I touch & see

an accretion of excess
fuel first dumped
then evaporated from
above the low

scuttled tone
of your voice associative
processes
of a bowling ball
properly squeezed &
released from the service area up

into expectant palms

he was drawn
to immersive things

mouths without
faces faces
without eyes media
absent mediation

like adolescence but better
a fold in clothing or the skin
we watch only what we can
scroll our impression
of keeping time

witness my démodé
wears your hankering
for rough
cut & sluggish
we correlate
with "authentic"
& "spontaneous"
            wait slow down
we wanted (a bigger splash)

thrumming synth parenthesis
paves a new breath your neck shapes
like swans in the periphery
            is this real
is this real & did I take it
like a man

{who's the boss}

lulling touch of familiarity
if I place my hips here

an accident of shadow
where you enter the frame

I feel some
kind of way about it

you mouth & I want
to fill your mouth

with confectioner's sugar
I ask servers

to omit on hotcakes
such embarrassment of seeing

the text behind emoji
instead of unalloyed emoji

such embarrassment of seeing
your space heater in my day

dream I was the curtains
we just glided past

in the club that gluts
our crotches in advance

who's the boss?
not a question or come-on

but the set we've each
wandered upon

"camera men" thrusting
lenses in our non-specific

vicinity dream we are each
ablaze between the singularities

get it? inertia
of my late tuesday

morning in the middle
of my life I came to myself

within a stretch of subway
ads hiss of a train's brake

to remind me I've just
missed out I am missing out

but for twitter to tell
me you are all

caught up I am catching
another train I am copping

a feel in my daydream
downtown F hallucination

in which we inch
closer & take turns

on duolingo
german becomes french becomes

clandestine juices held
on the tongue

a woman wants me to know
the world is full of paper

could this account I wonder
for the upswing of bad poems

in the world not recent
but rather "timeless"

dilemma the same
woman wants me

to tell her the secret of my tan
my secret is the color

of my skin I want to say
the color of all the poems

in the world before
they were poems & all the poems

to be had
or mishandled notion

of the "sweaty carpet"
riddle of the sphinx

in a children's picture book
riddle of your crown

on my head
trauma of my coronation

as alternate title
your palm against the cool

metallic arm with which
we will flush this down

& watch each couplet swirl
as deleted scene

no inertia without gravity
no gravity without

your socks
in my drawer

intensity of every eye contact
when it's unintended & what

it might ever entail
satisfactions of the brand-new brita

my mustache in a public place
malfunction of these steamed buns

vacations that mean something
vacations & eye contact & dim sum & dante & space

heaters & flush
as the electric feeling

in my cheeks
before we

squirt I want to
be the cheek & the tissue

& the tear / theorem
the sun sets

in the east
but where is my face

when you are
kneeling

where is your face
when I am being fed

{candy risks}

probable bodies this island
as contrapuntal every
several years I revive

in syndication even my skull
candy risks
expiration in public

transitioning from pup
to dream
phone boy on your screen

I die into last
night's well
rehearsed instructions

you compliment
my vascularity guess
we each have skin

in the game
I comb bushes
for hints these

grubhub ads arouse
I've been told
my taste

rides thick the mouth
as a seat of worship
joy mirth music

{repeat since you want immersion}

in light of portico
fatigue you invite
me to your tennis
club. the rally

was as deliberate
as a twitter thread
all the poets chanting representation
without commodification

business as usual
exchanging one
colonial tongue
for another

while I window
shop the women's section
of prada bc gender
this evening I am

rapacious scribe
reciting original
lyrics at my local
gelateria. together

we watch jill biden
pronounce "bodega"
on repeat. since
you want immersion

in agony we meet
at the museum
one man on a horse with a hat
my desired minimum

length. later
we will make
an offering
to dionysus in

a cave. my face
up against an opposite
corner & other acoustic
phenomena. the speaker

in a roman fresco. the train
will soon depart
it was inconvenient to live
in a tower. traditionally

they pour it on the hand where
it is licked clean. some colors
are ingrained in memory
anonymous portrait of women

beating hemp in hungary
using blue to make yellow more
yellow. I trust
myself less & less

he has a soft
spot for "foreigners"
we are doing this
at high speeds

{prufrock's ball}

lather the aloe
now you

ask nicely
round & round

my widening gyre
jasön certified

organic taste
test means

I can rub it
on my skin

& also use my tongue
safe to say

I grind
my own coffee

cutthroat world
of the arts & letters

to rilke on my
to-do list

everything depends
on a swollen thigh

redolent with cream
as a verb aspirations

on a first date
someone's seventh

floor roof deck
our taut polaroid

the wind & your palm
in my hair

multimedia rendering
of prufrock's

society ball
I was the only one

wearing shorts
asking whether

metal sweats
in the tropics

inside my cheeks there
is a poem forming

I burned the top
of my mouth for this

{picturing my present}

in a blurb everyone
is having fever dreams
& a rare & singular voice

the amount of sweat my ass
cultivates in august is literally
beneath me

you might be picturing my secret
bath the way I am
picturing my present

groping for waste

{forever chemicals in our rainwater}

rendezvous inside frederick
the great's beloved
"china room"

sometimes I require
great abandon not
everyone has an ass

fetish commodity
they read marx
"in the original"

my mustache trimmer
arrives posthaste
splice the meaning

of our hobbyhorse
do not go
gently into this

google hangout lay
the cutlery meant
for entertaining

now my scepter
should remain merely
curiosity an impulse

to reconstruct
typos in the second
edition such

a thing as forever
chemicals in our rainwater
we had lost all feeling

of time

{prone to domination}

we cool our heels in the fat one
interlude as brief as this
fugue in flight enter

-tainment under the arches
once we've been
made nude

descending a fire
escape (no. 2)
sitting on the rim

align the anus
with the column
of spray water

here come the warm
jets laid over this morning
prayer a vision of brian

applying ointment
to each armpit
my t.j. maxx activewear

smells of your product
your product smells
of a cognate

for myrtle
I prefer my body's
dominant leg

folded against my
leg deemed less prone
to domination

gathering this intel
under the table
we assume other covers

for my onlyfans
I recite althusser
from memory

garbed in lard
sculptor's robe in the so
called artist district

you tout your suite
of unrhymed sonnets
my ragu achieves

homage as
"unbecoming"
how to use a bidet

with images
among the most
popular searches

geolocation my innuendo
hard to shake how
her tomatoes looked

better remember everything
beloved must
first endure

abasement
I was so full
of shame before you

gave me my eyes

{my disobedient cowlick}

first I fold
my tongue over
the sticky crease
& seal this

message like a piñata
sampling brute
force & gritty
confidence to drag

& drop then caress you spray
tan I polish
my turmeric
stained cutlery as

a boy I wanted
only to be a cloud
eater she requested dressing
"on the side" we resisted

my paywall you shouldn't
take yourself
so seriously like this
better with music &

distance by design
daily disposed to maneuver
my disobedient cow
lick the mirror

scene in conan
the destroyer lu/ore
of my expansion
pack you wanna

74

have your cake &
me to bust
from the very top
I trumpet the thumb

nail parade
on my back
alley wonder
when you read this text

mispronouncing insouciance
my whole life
yt folks wish for me
to know my ideas

hold merit

{this form of wood}

google imaging or just imagining nervous wall
street traders always makes me
feel so much

better knowing I'll never make anything
except my own desire
to be destroyed in the flesh

I am merely a commodity that hasn't
transcended sensuousness
& so I'll stand on my head

if you will take your
place against my back
& sit

{secret cinema}

what the eye wants & what the mouth wants what the mind wants
& what memory wants what the hands

want & the feet want what the thighs want what the hips want
what the lips the teeth the tongue want

what the torso wants & what the neck wants what the buttocks
wants what the prayer wants & the

forgiveness & the blessing what the asshole wants what the face
wants what the space between vulva &

anus wants what the double-parked fedex delivery driver wants
what the envelope wants & the thumb

pressed against the paper what the shaft wants & what the head
wants what the theater wants & what

the reel wants what the projectionist & the family camcorder want
what the suction & cylindrical rim want

what the vacuum of representation wants what the wet & writhing
wants the fingers the palm the labia the eye

lid the grunt & collapse what the bent over & rocking wants what
the spray of ejaculation wants the all

in one shampoo & conditioner wants what the thought of it
(turning me in a circle in the night / like

a fire) cup of dawn & my hands inside my jeans wants what the
zipper wants what the undressed window

wants what the apparition fanning out across the glass wants what
the arched back the cocked chin the drizzled

nipples want what the electronic message wants (asking to distill
this / asking to expand) what the crossed

& uncrossed limbs want & what the oil wants what the fist wants
& what the stroke of redaction

wants what the studied pose wants & the leaking frenzy of your
emission what the touch wants before

the feel what the smell of humming along the skin wants what the
bitmap graphic & the lick of thumbnail

eloping & the audio we'll add later over & out over & out over &
out below or inside the shock of reception

in the throat the unrehearsed stutters & groans what the quiet
wants what the close-up wants what the sticky undissolvable

silence

{when news telecasts turn over}

watching the 2000s on CNN
gives me more

anxiety than living in the 2000s
the compulsion to keep

watching plays to my desire
to relive the apocalypse

of youth & yet
when news telecasts turn over

fifteen years old they also
turn into lo-fi soap

operas you want to
know why I say

it's the alchemy
of asynchrony

{your new & selected rolodex of taste}

on the internet I rent
a swimming pool

in lisbon with a black russian
terrier at my side

your new & selected
rolodex of taste

-ful "food porn" please
acknowledge my hair

on the beach
looks better than

my hair off the beach
despite beach-dried locks

belonging on my to-do list
before our date I dry

my mane with man-made
blow amid

my fear
of belatedness

still deep in throes
of this recitation

beside my duplicate I actualize
our stage directions

first unpeel the guanabana
then admire its pleasing

bouquet on a scale of 1 to 10
how papal do you want me

to look on my screen
meet the soviet superdog

{I want your hand roll}

moments before the press
screening we practice

lifting our legs first
grab the back

of each ankle
etymology of fluent

here I want your hand
roll belly flown

in from central tokyo south
bound on the train

to aix I jettison
a stowaway fashion

myself a mistress
rococo

on the inside install
a linen skirt

to my mainframe
debut my new factory

settings a prayer
of the rollerboys

blonde like 1990
patricia arquette

undercover asset passing
as straight to video

{they paid to have their face removed}

overcast my favorite
setting from this
cushioned distance
I can water the surface

of each leafy crown these
red bricked
domes of prayer &
murmur an indecipherable

horizon or passing
swarm of subway cars to alter
the range of light &
select a second

gradient wrecked
by the arrangement
of potted plants before
the blue ruin

an earnest kernel
error my machine
stutters again against
your unrolled sea

weed algae shredded
& then hung
dry reminded then
we cast glances

at our virtual tour
ceremony of the sommelier

first swirl then sniff
your american standard

toilet with its economy
splash pattern my solar
plexus gurgles awaiting
I absorb you

fancy yourself
size queen
I gyrate to castles
in the sky my

neck wreathed in neon
glow so conjure
the late eighties
trope cross-dress

to consummate secret
heterosexual fantasy
I clad myself
in jock strap

you left my sweat
towel there to
invite crowd
sourced collaboration

we wrote a self
portrait as others
see us your image
stirs up both

expectation & memory
in leather
jacket speed
walking through nolita

people call me the latino
jason bourne after
the "pain-free" procedure
they paid to have their face

removed from all search
engines first we consent
to our own subjugation
trick of the eyes

I fasted for forty
breaths before you
prompted me to buzz
you up I too

was onboarded
only after several brief
interrogations mystic
river bed teeth

of a dog my tarot
mistress mining crevices
for hard-earned crypto
inspire me to probe

the girth of my deep
end & the unseen
musculature I want to honor
your roughage

rip you
an exit theme
to aid these calisthenics
feeling all the heat

leaving my hips upon
careful consideration

I've gone too
far before edging

myself into another
shaking fit taking
solace knowing my tense
unraveling in the family

bathroom at the bottom
of the sixth was not my most
egregious misstep
turning your mouth

into a fountain at the height
of my desire to be
received whereupon she
conducted her

careful assessment
my trade
in value
but I can

always morph
reality
what else is a poem
here for

{under your humming palm}

you reek of trust
fund aesthetics I piss on
men for money
a fist full
of cashews for a film
reformatted as easy
jet entertainment
best western
waterbed for pam & tommy
master tapes miracle
of conversion you
can't escape
geography & the world
bank internet barter
paul walker
laying in hay
I sat here
under your humming palm
tree refresh
my page entreats
a long load
distinction between eating
pasta salad & writing
a pantoum never have I ever
sucked a mentos
to completion

{the e-commerce high}

everywhere I go I
ask for victuals off
the menu

victoria from ukraine
my preferred dental hygienist
picturing my face

during routine oral
checkup a reverse
turn-on picturing

my blush banana
republic chinos
against your chin for

comfort & reliability
at the e-commerce high
fashion fête I wear cargos

& eastern bloc era tank
reverence < irreverence
want to relish all

seven deadly sins
where to kill is to join you
in reciprocal orgasm

would like
to be remembered
for the sound of my

thighs clacking against
your negative space
my conviction

the best poems
written in half
a day or less

-er known fantasy
of orpheus
rehearsing hot yoga

at my dining table
curious minds ask
about the way I break

truth
or dare my proof
is in the pudding

{spilled mezcal > spilled milk}

reviving this
fuzzy hand-held
gaze we could circle

time in ink angel
of history head
turned always toward new

jersey incorporated
townships in your
dream I fancy

myself a shop boy
hurling dime
store orchids at the fountain's

edge konsumterror's
fleshy wreckage we peruse
frankfurt school in newark

airport parable
of the skymall one single
catastrophe

grand opening
of the hawaiian room
concept of the sweet nothing

I named my holy ghost after
man with the strongest
pour

a tautology wasn't
then it was
his spirit was in my low balls

days hence
something here
is taking shape

king cobra > cobra kai
swivel arm battle
grip body

design as my first
stimulus package
nascent subjectivity an eager american

voice I try in vain to emulate
naming poets for the smells
we give off

naming gelatos for your celebrity
chefs before & after
the scene of their crime

as method & correspondence
at the banya I fall
pray to the god

of skin tingle & white borsch
several sudden hands
gesturing mid steam

sometimes you only see a thing
if you put it out there
entelechy sometimes

I practice pronunciation
on the internet before I am
asked to speak

epanalepsis people
also search for
empanada mama your shirt

says I can't believe I ate
the whole thing
my shirt says spilled

mezcal > spilled milk
atop revolving stage
my shame at asking

for a taxi on the street
idea of hailing / being
hailed "with time

[   ] was everywhere"
my operatic confession < your invitation
to join my dojo

andrei serkolov gives
the best massages my
unsaved contacts

give the best
messages detail
of the mutual flute I inhaled

your verso some
say a religious experience
I repeat you back

the right horse
we got your chase
quick deposit I ask

the audience
which song plays
if you are entering

a room slowly
walk toward me
make whole all

that is hidden

{time while desire}

a friend wants to
know so I tell a friend
the real secret

to honest
praise is writing
about your own

work then
substituting
another's name

moral or myth
of plymouth rock
my skipping

stone's uncertain
dispersal against
the throat so

ruminate hardness
& strength versus softness &
flexibility

I traffic head
set memories another
disappointing eclipse

clad in daddy's
cummerbund
we exchange assassination

coordinates
what a mirror misses
but movement

my way of walking through
a room as on a
street my way

of meeting you
a single stroke on a
single day seen & not since

forgotten
the idea & the story
of the idea / in the story

every moment
a consequence of another
moment / fiction as a form

of accountability
in the real / desire
we measure like measuring

time while desire
would like
only to keep

watch

{the verbal british fantasy}

I remember the dew on your cheeks
I remember the places he lived &
was loved
feel the shiny silver
globe & pluck it from my hip
it is dark though early
afternoon as I enter your video
parlor but before I press
your feet with the rounded
edge of my head
the joy of handling < implied touch

your vertical
thrust & the knowing
of it wait
of your polygonic torso in the cup
of my thumb & weight
of the breath pursed against
my drumming lips
foam-flecked amidst
the crush of this
rhythmic exactitude
since every wandering conceals
its purpose
since I've already memorized
all my openings

despite knowledge to resist
spontaneous combustion
when we scuba mouthing
I am never not not
myself you
peddle virtues

of smallness versus
solidity & heft & cuisinart
14-cup processor's
extra-large feed tube
to endure the terror
of others we practice
gelatin recreate our
sleeves of flesh atop
mortar & pestle
decamp into unspecified present
words into letters into signs
or the reverse I
lost your dot dot dot

we play at the comma
unnaturally inserted
after our origin delay
embarrassment
for these imperial tendencies
a two bagged mango
daily regime we each
scatter against the flattened
surface of a vatic sacrum
confusing american
civil war for
my molecular dissolution
at a party

city / is that your hand there is that your
poem on that printed paper

cloaked in man-skin
my earth magic stokes
a roving platform's mechanical
transaction means we mimic
these movements to turn
the mealy exterior
of our purse's tokens

into amuse
bouche / barter
accents as we reconsider
the double s
in the verbal
british fantasy
so I spent a childhood
of farina mornings
gazing with care
fully crushed
sangfroid absent
a stranger's flaxen
nimbus & hair
on the box a promise
of creamy enrichment
as asshole urges
with archival inevitability

look the cheesecake
is sweating again

look I cloak myself in the common
guise of another
unthinking citizen & each
stressed syllable
of vanished graphic

{trying hard is beneath you}

& on my seventh day
job we
bypass our server

recommends stomach
the flesh
from the bone my

keeper of mp3s
we make visual
situations I kazaa

this revision
crave illicit
trespass plumb

an avatar's meek patina
you pronounce yourself story
of the eye & the gut

doctor begs
every american throw out
this vegetable

now new
to this world
& the husk

I squat
inside trying
hard is beneath

you apply to
be my witness nostalgia
for cold war urban

planning I like
the specificity of this
scenario remember how

we crawl the touch
tunnel the way
you trace me

by the spit I offer
as token & receipt toggle
between childhood/s

enlarged impression
of depth from distance
throat my memo's

audiobook a guttural
remedy if oil
is drilled from

the body an invitation
for durational performance
absent missionary

we antioxidize
sam's club cacao your
appendices burst

with self
citation young
skin runs

in my family
fragility of the first
briefly sketched image

asked to imagine
what may have taken
place you feel

my fake
nudes making
the rounds again

take turns down
my caribbean cask
purloin the fabric

intended for swaddling
an infant we consider
tapas I favor

gamier mammals
the exact description
was a sucker

for aromatics
summoned to rinse the mullet
your extract & hip

waft an echo
the dolphin my first
virtual companion together

we forage our core
before the layer
of crust bubble

the vapor seeking
a surface I demo
a glossy

legend below
the text for
our safety

words get off
to action / adventure
sprites we join

skins in quest
mode members
only thirst

for yours I sliver
web 2.0 into tercets
use my roommate's face

wash for the novelty

{pay my garden gnome}

indeterminacy of appetites
under this disco ball
plays across the body

consumes & is consumed
collecting my pearls
on the club floor

expression of the juice
my ascending sign
the human use of human faces

a slug's muscular fluctuations
language without speech
a bundle of hand

pulled noodles
slapped lengthened
& slurped slow motion

we dance the lipsi
indulge my dacha
pay my garden

gnome a visit
you pen
your signature

in my hausbuch
I open the pail
& pull out the words

red like the inside
of a body
the secret

police label us
"negative decadent"
ask me if I like this

unprovoked riddle
how many antechambers does it take
to access the center of my inner sanctuary

survey my preference
to be served
I beckon you

eat me à la française
play taylor swift
to my roland barthes

unspeakable heap
of flesh you wear
short skirts I wear

jean shorts seek
vertical thrills
glances stolen satellite

television commission
my panorama your bitcoin
back-to-back we

each impaled
aboard identical
armchairs

{jump on a call with me}

what's the difference between a guest & an uninvited guest an un-
invited guest & a guest that comes too late

to be as well-loved
as goethe is by eckermann
to have even my wrinkles

speak with such expression
as goethe's fine lines
do for eckermann

to eat grapes from
my master's hand
is to edge

closer to be
as near as I
will ever get

as for example
what you imagine
when I ask you to

jump on a call
with me I am
wanting to be the one

on the call & also
to be the phone colloquially
jumped on

{unattainable in this ruby tuesday}

between our first
act & the third
I golden

hour your navel
partial to a 3 to 1
aspect ratio his AI

avatars harvest
an extra set of legs my own
affinity to be stroked

by unrecognized & decussating
palms can't you
tell I never

gave up this life
of puppy
dom at the cut

rate repast I request
my spread be served
with the heads on

I'll show you my data
set if you
show me yrs

that raw yet crispy salmon
unattainable in this ruby
tuesday so I aspire to leek

consciousness can I
melt with you can I
stop the world

my heartbeats
so far & few between
unless you ask

I catty-corner my quadricep
along the slat of flesh
that bears no name

remember not
all angels
have wings

where once was a nipple
is a tongue
let's indulge our unethical

curiosity to fall
silent as I absorb
the host

weren't we always
images of people
who did not exist

{gifted as interval}

I work with the body I have
seen on pamphlets shopfront
ads a roving graphic

ripples across the 11th
last night's mimetic cabaret
my feed a series

of street art screenshots
I wanted it & I enjoyed it & I knew
it was wrong meet me

in a hall of toilets
I spawn on command fascinated
by the automatic orange

presser at franprix &
later to bathe
incense a stranger

bottled & gifted
as interval course
"cleanser" people

who cannot see
colors can feel
skin's chroma

in other ways jazz
flame sea sky eyes
the difference

between accident & miracle as
blur a magic marker
makes could never be

born in a place so small so
I was born
here the only one

in all a person
can believe anything if squatting
to queue below the storied

arc like always
I wait for an opening
tingle of "frontispiece"

as shape insinuates surface
a galette's soft exit belatedly
insert interview & commentary

my shaking fits
the thrill of potential
a craving for couscous

sonic pleasures $\cong$ pleasures
of the flesh menemen
chakchouka lablabi hear

say the same breath inherited
on the page I read some
of us will retain form & some

of us will not everything
I feel is felt
at least twice

miracle
or accident? truth
be told I like a machine

beat better
even if I stretch inside
a crowded metro

petals on a wet black
beau leaning to be deeply
received beside

these apparitions or this
haiku's glazed sprint
repetition of dusted

canals my speaker
phone instructions untellable
heaving throat

as other
than a noun well
oiled plastic

sac I squeeze
out
a sigh

{& sky looked}

& there would be bedroom & queen bed & light gray walls that
look blue in evening & there would be

hand on screen finger on face face hovering over body's erasure &
there would be night before the night

just as seconds before the first just as consent to dissolve us into
dead time where each endure the long

slow glow of excess saturation & there would be waiting of words
before words & text before transmission

& bubbles that signify thought coming inside or in between &
there would be language coming out from

skin & sensation. Over. Out. Just like that. & there would be film
s/playing & there would be music on

TV & there would be cool sweat forming across a brow on the
neck down the back between the thighs

& there would be mounted fan spinning in another room some-
where we couldn't be & there'd be two

people or one person looking at the other & the other looking
back & there would be the sign or slip to signify

REALPEOPLENOTACTORS

& window would be open & breeze would come in every other
moment & every other moment I'd be

thinking about it & thinking about it & thinking about how to live
inside instead of all the time above it & there

would be bedroom & queen bed & screen backlit & sky looked
like this from my viewpoint under

showerhead: & it felt so good & it feels so good & I am feeling & I
am being felt—*seen at 11:42 pm*—& I'd see

it again looking back because a glance (she knew) could be as
wide as an open mouth & I had a certain

desire to fade out into the scenery scanning with first my index
whereupon certain patterns should begin to

emerge for instance congruences between the total number of
people that drowned in a pool & the number

of films in which nicolas cage participated or the divorce rate in
maine & the per capita consumption of

margarine

{in a slippery body}

you woke up
like this
buffed & well-lit

as my omakase I feign
nervous excitement
procure us

a leitmotif
panoptic view
of the theater box < peephole

in a holiday
inn a slippery body
superimposed

on a swimming pool's
mute surface
exerting effects

on the viewer "willy-nilly"
say sight
becomes obstacle

to sensation
my memory jogs
traces of your g-string

this commute a cradle
of relief allowing myself
to be manipulated

by your composition
writing things without
knowing why

you emphasized
rivulet of lossy
compression my source

file you stream
from above they asked me to
make it two times

life-size to scale
we are eagerly awaiting
my peer review

all four obliques
of perspective
neck susceptible

to famine tap
twice the fleshy replica
back in manhattan

even my chalice
foams at the counter
labyrinth of the text

a casting couch
saliva your
keepsake we are

doing this on both
legs I forgive you
for doctoring

your face I forgive
myself for tasting
of jergens original

healing the milk
truck approaches our rear
as I hum your hymn this close

crop sweetens
my mirror
you mouth

full I fill
my syntax
looking to give

off sensodyne gentle whitening
muscles still
beating after the act

an encore we scope
bridge & tunnel mystique
basic like the questions

of sexuality
hesitation of shape
coming into focus

exhilarating nothing sound
carrying you around
in my body our

six-dollar thigh
& drum combo
we audition elven

smirk my fellowship
of the ring I kneel
to pocket applause

untrained like the best
poets I did not ride
here on a horse I pegged

you aboard citibike
lip copernicus while in orbit
you questioned balls

in your court
I say let's
make this real

{near the end of the world}

I watch the women
open when we meet

at baseline sport
a tyrolean hat

you heave I teach
you how to

gargle everything's coming up
rosés I hedge

my risk
free taste test

to look without
fear my

one talent
I burn

you a worthy
mood here

we near
the end of the whorl

of flesh made
word

{my mind inside your body}

she's trying too
hard again
we've figured
my secret
ambitions for the text
to be as easily
copied & parted
with as a pamphlet

(flashback to that
one week he had two
bad hair days)

desire brightening in
the tell
tale sign of bodily
prominence

I ask for my customary double
was I a call
boy then were you
my mistress mistaking
me in the radio
shack inaudibly
playing nasty boys
thinking if this

ever did happen
where would I be
where would I be now
-adays is not a day & neither
is a single simultaneous our
nonbinding agreement

we held our words open in an open
palm a pause
the hand
held see how light
flickers on his friend hard
to admit how

much I really liked it
the song's shimmering
chorus recall
janet chanting
sitting in the "movie
show" thinking
nasty thoughts
since this citation feels
necessary
how come we hear
the sound when we see

the image
so you can see us
buffer on your manus
on your coiled
thumb a care
free announcement

I'm a first timer I do both
domestic & international

"by hook or by crook"
the simple fact
of your asshole & did
I like it when I was being buried
beneath the humming
energy of an expanding
ozone back in slowly a sign
says back in

new jersey
fingered in the ridge
wood cinema till I come
matt damon saying
serious things clad
in leather think

I might have died
during the ultimatum
or been dead for far longer
maybe I'm still dead there
clutching a fountain

soda my seat
back resisting
an original position

(funny how the same god
paired this body with this
consciousness)

all the time we wonder who
is the speaker in the poem

it was his fingers I think it was
his hand on your knee

so it is by putting things inside
us that we can retrieve the rolls
of film even effortlessly

how this sounds different once you
record & then overlay
the copy that milk

ad adolescence
always aroused
stiffening under
the loose fabric
worn between
the genitals &
your mirror
to be so suddenly
tall & muscled
just by looking
a piece of sky patterns
of weather

(how impetuous the audience
they flit from one
deity to another)

your neck my wish
bone when we were
still tuning to this
instrument each brought
out anew
melodic strain in the other

(ankled in the mid
winter
& angular
& we kept making it
like this with
our mouth)

your need full
-ness my grip filled
with subtitled
indiscretions

so enter the dragon
& the wanting
a dragon brings

like try that trick again
how I put my mind
inside your body
or vice versa
how final it all is but I'm good
at stretching
a point
the perfect search
engine envisioned as the eye
of god

nothing causal
about this continuum & anyway
plastics are merging
with my organic particulates
again

(she made a face unsure
what kind)

your mood I might
call "conjunctive"
a break
in the trees allowing
the light to be
held in reverse so
common in dialogue
scenes every story occurring
on some other side
a linked fence the erotic
monotony of hedges

I make lists
array my vitamins
try to have
intentions

edge each other's innocence
flatten your hand & run
the fatty metacarpus
along my navel

something omitted here or vulgar
tendencies to refer to myself
in the second person

a muffled shared
snickering then
do I look
like someone

who would take
a taxi light
traffic the waists
of women & men
moving upward on a motorized
carpet dogs on ocean
leaning
with their tongues out
turn yellow turn
read my life
lived in some state
denial or improbable
optimism against which
everyone having to
"pull your weight"

but for his intermittent & immaculate
torso
jutted & obscene
in my gathering
thoughts no longer any
"mystery"
what we picture when we hear
the voice
see how anyone can play
this recorder

see how
servers on roller
skates juggle
plates like floating
saucers

we wrote a letter
I used his ears
& eyes

exchanging age
sex & echolocution
sing stolat
stolat my inherited
hymn may we live
a hundred years a hundred more

& if he pretends to check
his phone
during parties
if he pretends to be another
(as anything other
than what he is) this
private experience of writing
in public

derived as I am from each
east & west

& would I ever return

meaning suburban
setting a pool
side table chlorine jeans
rip slow & merciless in this
scenario I smell like we've been
swimming the real
fear is not appearing
as silken as
one's icon &
just as silent

they clamored for
the cover version
what war didn't
we come back from

disappointed to not learn
anything about the author upon
reading their autobiography
the old familiar itch
(he scratched
out the name & wrote
mine)

asking can I get his hair
do can I have a do-over

& then there was
audio again
there were sighs & grunts &
absurd disclosures in close
caption our reluctance

to ever meet
halfway our refusals
of redemption

admitting this distance
is nothing

{mannequin}

you flaunt your oranges
I came to

on the upper east
I was juan the buenas dias bellhop

arturo the cabana boy
stewart the bartender

jj the porn actor careful
not to improvise a star

you were the man
who fell in love with

his own mannequin
dressing

windows in moving
picture of the same

en un rincón de
mi mente microphone

in hand I divide
my film into

roll-calls *say*
my name say

my name
you search

for your "vocation"
I search my spotify

for "romance ballads"
two data points don't make a trend

two bodies don't make a double
penetration et cetera

I lap your orb for divinations
you feed me bona fide secrets

betrayal of the real
I am not

your carrier
pigeon

{this recalcitrant hair flip impulse}

retain my cheekbones
on camera evidence
my non-normative

copay opt in
memoriam glitter receipt
our ancestral odor drone

searching power
drill best practices
I have broader lips than most

clarion call of morning
breath we sketch
our terror for access

admiring an excessive
load I impatiently
harvest if these eye

lashes could talk your scenic
gopro vista vintage
lunchbox a lewk all ready

to wear me
reversible phishing up
stream blush we

peer recent back
light crop
bodied close shimmering

mother unseen inquiries
from the audience play
your process dust reflex

I lead a miraculous childhood
my mirror the first
opening I touch today time

your talkie camera stunt
before private detonation
neoliberally unencumbered

my cucumber
lemon cayenne cleanse
ritual mouth

feel your seed
skittish to jaw
out in the open

this recalcitrant
hair flip impulse
tattoo my passport

until likeness   skips
a scratch
on the record

{I forgot I was wearing you}

heaving under the stain
glass windows us &
every other body

made obscure by the fish
net mesh I forgot I was
wearing you pit

the difference
between indication &
expression identityless

like airport furniture
foreign objects fictional
stagings the phrase

make berlin
shit again above
the bill your military

debris chic drag
of recognition any
eye contact while

grinding me seen
as aggressive I reneged
my NDA a reputation

for being the hardest
house in the world the general
functionality of rims

asked to aestheticize
the humiliation of
being human unnaturally

catapulted across
the sky powdered
battery acid I have five

words for blue
paradoxes of high speed
travel's sense of comfort turn

myself fully to flight
mode a worn
in pair of hokas shiny

silver tin
packed flesh my economy
class legs perusing

acceptable risk
emancipation of the I
from the subject

or the reverse one
of these things
is not like the other

flex this
at a 33-degree angle
& find out

It's difficult to admit this bc we're afraid of ~~losing~~ ourselves. And this is what softened me. He began to feel my voice again in his mouth. The air was still. Birds were on the branches. Sound of tires under negative acceleration, a car pulling toward the curb, persons dropped or about to be, the drift of approach. Around the corner, another corner. The grating roar of Ocean, & beyond Ocean, the green-screen sea. I felt my eyes being sensational & wet. Remember? It was 7:07. At some point, a minute passes. It almost always does. Shocking doorbell footage shows saber-wielding burglar tasered by police. We waited for our oat milk latte. The way we wait for death. What else is there to say? I thought I could be a person. That, of being flesh, I could return us to the inside. Where we could remain unspoken for. That thing could be given form without its being given a word. Under the impression that the most dangerous gaze is the reflex to look back. In this mirror that catches everything against its slick surface, wall to wall, we retreat to an earlier pose. Pondering the resemblances between a copse & a thicket. What is mine isn't. What is yours if not me. The seed ripening already in the throat. I'm gonna lay here on the grass, you typed back, & blow bubbles & shit. To look up with shock is to acknowledge the grandeur of paradise. Come to the window, sweet is the air. Look at us, repeating hymns we learned in high school. That unforgiving or unforgettable moment when I gave my life away. Steered clear of currency, I had my work, they boded, "cut out for me." Eleven hundred severed heads, each with symmetrical eyes, nose, & mouth, with respect to the ears. They wanted moments of "autobiography." + the failure of ever really knowing anyone. Was there a difference between sex & possession when the intention was to feel from your thumbs taste from your tongue see from your unblinking orifice. Consider the consequences of getting what you really want. And all this writing contaminated by ambition & the shame of holding a body that is not yours to own. The fear of coming clean, admitting that it's easier to play dead. My so-called life. The pleasure of pictures tending to atrophy any urge for action. Though it's better isn't it that we can hold this vantage point indefinitely. A deepening afterglow across mute distances. She says, can we just laugh, for a fucking minute. He says, I'm at the airport, hence developing a massive list of desires. Since we believe the simple fiction that we are already touching. And having already touched what more was there to do but dissolve. But for the what if of any good crush. I said didn't I the most interesting detail in any photograph is the thing you don't see. He was described as having a rainbow-like sway of colors. Eyes like ports, ass like shipwrecks. Sound stipples into illegible semitones, a stuttering long line of spray where terminal C meets the moon-blanched land, crossroads of watching & waiting. Sample sample sample sale. And each .wav splices unequally. Something in the air says the archive is passing hands again. Summon a stretching field that reaches the forest on a foggy morning at the advent of spring. Clouds of magpies that I'd "originally" mistook for crows. The grass appears wet, indicating that it had recently rained, & with the sky still gloomy I assumed it would happen again. If we consider the crime was the witnessing. The lack of restraint or the fact of one's capacity to offer everything but one's self. When better means the same. When sameness means unity. And the tacit agreement that nothing happens (nothing will ever happen). Begin, & cease, & then again begin. All scenarios reducible to a common theme. + the error of equating description with intimacy. I held out bc I wanted to make this last. I withdrew bc I wanted to show myself, to see myself anew. And now, above my head, witness a cartoon garland of stars. And now I'm coming up again, as if for breath. I wonder though. How does one, your text said, get used to having arms. Why do cookies turn hard. Ppl also ask why do hearts turn hard. Why the muscle tenses to anticipate touch, why the mind quickens for the clutch of vertical lines. & their jagged distribution across a shore. He was looking for a place to store our memories. The air was still & the windows rolled low, so my free hand reached out to meet the dying sun. Turn yellow turn red. It's all over for us, except for my dangling legs, the flexion of rib cage as I integrate respiration. Except for these trees, the sound of cars slowing to a halt, hauling rubber against the road littered with receipts. Birds sitting on their branches. Except for the analgetic violence of any dream that likes to perch on high. We were trying to outlive forever. Since what makes us human is our human misery. & this is what softened me, softened us. That nothing is mine not even me. Not even the sudden weakness in the skin that means my image is fleeing again, forgetting to drag the body that bears it. A person dropped or about to be. I began to feel his voice again in my mouth. And the screen is calm tonight, the screen is calm tonight the screen is calm tonight the screen is calm

Acknowledgments

Thank you to my friends and family, without whom *Windows 85*, and most of my writing, would not exist. I'm especially grateful to early readers of these poems, mentors and accomplices who continue to challenge and inspire me: Lilly Wu, Jason Zuzga, Miciah Hussey, Jay Gao, Reuben Gelley Newman, Ryan Cook, Jennifer Soong, Rockwell Harwood, Wayne Koestenbaum, Chris Hosea, Matt Broaddus, Chen Chen. The epigraph from Severo Sarduy's *Pájaros de la playa* was translated into English by Jill Levine and Carol Maier and published by Otis Books / Seismicity Editions as *Beach Birds* in 2007. The second epigraph comes from the 1995 film *Johnny Mnemonic*, which was directed by Robert Longo and written by William Gibson, who adapted his 1981 short story. The image of window cleaners in Lisbon that graces this book's cover was photographed by Nuno Silva. The interior image of people crossing the pedestrian lane in Tokyo was photographed by Samuel Scrimshaw. Thank you, also, to the editors and readers of the following journals, where the poems collected in this book, sometimes in different versions, first appeared:

"trinitarian formula," "unattainable in this ruby tuesday," "in a slippery body," and "mannequin," *Prelude* (2024)

Parts of "resource kit," "witness how time dilates," and "we've installed a new roof," *Tupelo Quarterly* 32 (2024)

"what vanna white sees in her sleep," *Sonora Review* 82 (2024)

Parts of "we've installed a new roof," "as natural as the camera," and "my mind inside your body," *Revel* 2 (Summer 2024)

"paul klee lives on," "water running in place," and "forever chemicals in our rainwater," *mercury firs* 5 (Summer 2024)

Parts of "trying hard is beneath you," *The Brooklyn Rail* (July/August 2024)

ROOF BOOKS

the best in language since 1976

Recent & Selected Titles